Advance Praise for Kirsten Grove and *Simply Styling*

"Kirsten's eye for design and style combined with her focus on creating comfortable, relaxing spaces is both refreshing and inspiring. You will love this book—it's a visual feast!"
—Holly Becker of *decor8*, Author and Stylist

"Kirsten has a rare capability to make spaces look simultaneously relaxed and refined. Her sensibility for mixing old with new, including contrasting shapes, unusual compositions and just the right amount of quirk makes her work simple and understated, without being boring."
—Justina Blakeney, Designer and Author, *The New Bohemians*

"I've long admired Kirsten Grove. One of the most loving and honorable women I know, Kirsten puts as much heart and soul into her interior design work as she does her family and community. This book reflects that character and inspires readers to find the soul of their own homes."
—Victoria Smith, Editor and Publisher, *sfgirlbybay*

"The very definition of the word 'simply' means straightforward and uncomplicated. Through the gorgeous, uncluttered images in this book, Kirsten very lucidly shares her expertise with all of us in both an inspirational and attainable way."
—Barb Blair, Author, *Furniture Makeovers* and *Furniture Makes the Room*

"Kirsten has such a fresh, hip and current take on interior spaces. She is able to transform rooms effortlessly and without any excess. Kirsten has the unique ability to edit down to exactly what both the interior and inhabitant really want and then style it flawlessly. This book provides so many unique ideas for pulling interiors together that it is sure to become a primer for styling modern spaces."

—Christiane Lemieux, Founder Lemieux et Cie, Founder DwellStudio, Author, *The Finer Things* and *Undecorate*

Simply Styling

Simply Styling

FRESH & EASY WAYS TO
PERSONALIZE YOUR HOME

KIRSTEN GROVE *of* SIMPLY GROVE

STERLING
New York

🌳
STERLING
New York

An Imprint of Sterling Publishing Co., Inc.
1166 Avenue of the Americas
New York, NY 10036

ISBN 978-1-4549-1822-6

Distributed in Canada by Sterling Publishing Co., Inc.
c/o Canadian Manda Group, 664 Annette Street
Toronto, Ontario, Canada M6S 2C8
Distributed in the United Kingdom by GMC Distribution Services
Castle Place, 166 High Street, Lewes, East Sussex, England BN7 1XU
Distributed in Australia by Capricorn Link (Australia) Pty. Ltd.
P.O. Box 704, Windsor, NSW 2756, Australia

For information about custom editions, special sales, and premium and
corporate purchases, please contact Sterling Special Sales at 800-805-5489 or
specialsales@sterlingpublishing.com.

Manufactured in China

2 4 6 8 10 9 7 5 3 1

www.sterlingpublishing.com

Book Design by Anna Christian

LIFE IS LIKE
A MOVIE,
WRITE YOUR
OWN ENDING.
KEEP BELIEVING.
KEEP PRETENDING.

JIM HENSON

why
HELLO

Contents

Foreword

Have you ever stopped to wonder, what is style? It can be a difficult thing to quantify. Is it how someone dresses? Or how they decorate their house? Sometimes style has a name like modern, eclectic or traditional. Sometimes style seems to defy definition. Many of us spend years trying to find our style, as if we were trying on dress after dress at a department store, always hunting for that perfect fit but never quite feeling comfortable with our selection.

Then there are those simply born with a distinct point of view. We all have one of those friends. The one with an inexplicable sense of what works and what doesn't. It's like they are part of a secret style society with a manual the rest of us aren't privy to. A plume of cool literally follows in their wake.

Kirsten Grove is a card-carrying member of that secret society. Style seems to ooze from her pores and I didn't even have to meet her in person to know that. Her blog, Simply Grove, sucked me into her modern yet casual, sophisticated yet approachable, cutting edge but timeless world long before Kirsten and I ever met in person. And when our paths finally did cross IRL (at a design blogging conference of course!), my suspicions were confirmed. She is cool, personified.

So when I heard Kirsten was going to bottle up some of her fabulous taste into book form, I was over the moon. For those of us who need a little extra guidance down the path to our own style holy grail, Kirsten is generously giving us 224 number of pages of design eye-candy that inspire, inform and let's be honest, give us serious house envy. But it's ok. If I can crib a few notes from Kirsten's style handbook, I know I—and the new house we just moved into—are going to be better for it.

Because style is never static. Even if you think you've got your look down, you always want to be searching for that next great source of inwspiration. I'm here to tell you, you've found it!

xo

Erin Hiemstra

Apartment 34

Introduction

I've always had a passion for interior design . . . well, at least since I was 9 years old and had free reign to decorate my bedroom. Back then, I was all about eclectic palettes of rainbows, polka dots, and stripes, using whatever I had to create my own personal oasis. Although now I've taken to a more streamlined aesthetic to design, the idea that I could transform a space and make it my own simply with what I had has always stuck with me.

The misconception about styling is that you need an endless bank account to achieve your desired look. Yes, if we all had money trees growing in our backyards we could have the space of our dreams. But I'm here to tell you that personalizing your home can be easy . . . and inexpensive. By using objects you probably have laying on your kitchen table right now, you can create eye-catching décor you never thought possible. And I'll show you just how in the following pages!

My personal philosphy is to live comfortably without sacrificing style. A comfortable space filled with personal touches can be fresh, exciting, and accessible. Before we learn how to achieve the unpretentious simplicity of great style in your home, let's first look at interior design in an out-of-the-box way that will help you visualize the spaces in your life with new inspiration.

Let's visualize your home as a song. I'm a music lover, which means there's a constant stream of music playing in my heart, in my head, and sometimes in my actual eardrums. Music has the ability to set the mood in every environment we encounter. What if your home were not only a reflection of your personal style but also a visual song that set the mood you wanted to live in?

When I catch a glimpse of great interior design, it's as if all the elements contribute perfectly to the overall tone of the space. Rhythm is one of the essential elements of music, and it's also a key ingredient to great design. It's the perfect balance of space and sound. Patterns and placement can activate or clutter space, and this book will help you

achieve a balance that soothes. When the rhythm is off in a song, it's blaringly obvious. One small tweak in styling can change the entire mood of the song—or the feel of a room.

Think about some of your favorite songs and how they make you feel. If it's a fresh, pop radio tune with catchy lyrics, what would that look like in a living space? Maybe it would be a bright, light, and airy room with fun patterns, filled with pillows you've collected over the years. How about an indie folk sound with driving rhythm? That would probably involve a contemporary, rustic feel with lots of natural wood elements.

I first found my song when I was super young. I remember visiting Portland in grade school and recognizing modern architecture and design. It was something that always made sense to me. After I graduated high school, friends and family members started asking me to decorate their homes. I used these moments as opportunities to grow and learn. Friends will always tell you if you've made a bad decision, and fortunately they will always forgive you for it.

Because I am self-taught, I have had to work hard to prove my talent. Whether it was working for builders or styling a baby shower, I strived for perfection. I didn't always gain perfection, but I set the bar really high for myself. It also helped me hone my ideas about design. I started specializing in restyling spaces with a smaller budget. I wanted both to have design be accessible and to inspire clients with fresh and evolving design. All of this creative energy spilled into my blog, Simply Grove.

It was an organic decision to start the blog. A friend planted the idea in my head, and I jumped at the chance. Because of putting myself out there, I have had many opportunities that still shake me in my boots. I remember when my first out-of-state client hired me. They asked to fly me to their city so that I could help them with a three-day styling project. I jumped at the chance and gave it my all. I have fallen many times, but it's been worth it.

You can't learn without making mistakes along this journey.

Fast-forward to today. I am styling homes all over the United States, e-designing for global clients, writing for influential design sites, constantly working with brands, writing for my own blog, and writing this book—not to mention raising two beautiful children and being married to the most handsome fella.

My own home . . . or soundtrack . . . is sprinkled with eclectic and traditional pieces, travel finds, and Scandinavian style. On the following pages, I'll teach you how to achieve your own unique and personalized home much like mine. It will be simple and inviting, bold and comforting. It is my joy and God-given dream to help you create a home that will instill happiness and peace every time you step through your front door. Come with me as we expand your mood board to include a soundtrack of inspiration to help style your spaces to perfection!

Living Room

Living Room

For most people, the living room represents a space for family and friends to gather and spend time together. It becomes a place to watch movies or your favorite TV series. Deep conversations are born here. Low-key dinner parties start and end in the living room. Living rooms bring people together. This is why it's so important to design a living space that is comfortable and easy to live in. It needs to be a place where you can put your feet up without feeling like you are going to offend someone. When I was a little kid, occasionally my family and I would eat dinner in the living room while watching *Jeopardy!* or *Wheel of Fortune*. Sometimes the meal consisted of Hot Pockets®; other times it was meatloaf and steamed carrots. I loved every moment of those laid-back nights.

A living room isn't just a formal place where you display your grandma's vases and knickknacks. It's a room that should reflect you and your household. Even in the most stylish spaces, a sense of comfort should be evident. My husband and I purchased the coolest midcentury chair a few years back. When it was delivered to our house, my husband sat in it and immediately had a sore bum from the weird angles and harsh lines. Needless to say, it only lasted a few months and was then listed on Craigslist® with ease.

Living rooms should reflect personality and taste. If you love color, introduce color to this space. If you are an avid book reader, create a reading nook. Live with what you love.

Note: Small spaces sometimes require the room to do double-duty. If you have your office in your living room, no problem! Just make sure to keep your desk tidy. Use beautiful containers that can store the practical things.

Main areas of your living room to be styled:

1 Coffee Tables

2 Mantel

3 Sofa

4 Accent Tables

5 Walls

6 Sideboard/
Entertainment Center

7 Vignettes

8 Shelving

9 Rugs

10 Lighting

1 Coffee Tables

Coffee tables can hold a lot more than just coffee. Whoever created the first coffee table created a masterpiece. It's one of those needed details that almost every living room requires. You can use your coffee table to display books, magazines, candles, and even plants. One tip is to style your coffee table in simple zones. Zone one can be a stack of magazines, zone two a large candle, and zone three a smaller plant. Or for larger coffee tables, zones one, two, and three can be stacks of books and zone four can be a wider yet smaller plant. Don't know what to do with your remotes or other practical items? Place them in baskets with lids or wooden bowls.

Height is an important factor with coffee tables. If you are looking over the table toward a TV, you will need your coffee table accessories to be low. If you are wanting a more sophisticated table, you can add some height with items such as candles and pottery.

A simple trick to give a coffee table or ottoman a mini makeover is to throw a vintage blanket over the top. It gives it an instant relaxed, bohemian look.

You can create collections on your coffee table, such as brass candle holders, ceramics, jars, books, magazines, or air plants. An easy way to keep the articles in the collection distinct is to display the items on a tray. This way you leave no stragglers behind.

When you are styling a square coffee table, try to mix in items that are round and rectangular to bring in dimension. The same applies to round coffee tables—choose square and rectangular items.

2 Mantel

When we think of mantels, we can have a tendency to think in traditional home terms. Things like gold frames and blue floral vases fill mantels all over the world. With a few styling tips, you can freshen up your mantel in no time.

Choose items that differ in height. For instance, if you have a tall plant, make sure you have a shorter item that can be paired with the taller item.

Art is the perfect backdrop for your mantel design. You can either lean art or hang it a few inches above the mantel.

For a simple look, create a small collection on your mantel. Display only a handful of small vases or small plants. This assemblage looks great on ornate mantels that don't need a lot of fluff.

Items to add
to your mantel:

1   Art

2   Plants

3   Ceramics

4   Candles

3 Sofa

There seems to be endless options when it comes to choosing a sofa. Once you walk into a shop or browse images online, the styles, shapes, and customization alternatives can become overwhelming. The last thing you want is to purchase a sofa and have it not be perfect for you and your family. Before you start the search, consider the tips on pages 16–21.

A throw blanket adds texture where there is none. Drape one over your sofa (or a chair) for a dose of color and texture.

How to style throw pillows:

1

Display pillows in groups of odd numbers such as one, three, or five.

2

To create variation, mix patterns with stripes and solids. Or have one pattern with two solids. Or include two striped pillows with a solid and two patterned throws.

3

For three pillows, display one on the left side and two on the right side. For five pillows, have three on the left and two on the right. For one pillow, place it in the middle of the sofa or on either side.

Sofa Tips

Let these simple tips help you find the right sofa.

size and shape

Size and shape come first. If you are looking for a comfortable sofa that you'll use for lounging, you'll want a deeper sofa. Standard sofa depths range from 36 to 38 inches. If you are taller or you anticipate using the sofa for curling up, opt for an even deeper version. If the sofa will be used more for an occasional sitting area, consider a smaller sofa or love seat. One way to easily determine the size you need is to cut out a paper template in the size and shape of the sofa you are considering and place it on the floor where the sofa will go.

 *upholstery*

Choose an upholstery that will best suit you. Aesthetic is important, but functionality is key when it comes to choosing a material for your sofa. For instance, suede can be a poor choice if you have pets or small children who will cause some damage. Leather is consistently in style, generally wears well with age, and can be easy to clean. Just be careful with the shape that you choose. Choose a leather sofa that is more streamlined than pouffy. If you choose a fabric upholstery, double-check that it has been treated and can be spot cleaned.

style

Style and comfort can go hand in hand. Knowing your personal style helps when trying to narrow down your search for the perfect sofa. Choose a style that reflects your lifestyle. If you lean toward more formal or traditional, a sofa with tufting or a tailored upholstered piece would be a great option. If you are more casual, a slipcover sofa makes a less formal statement and is great for high-traffic areas. Just throw it in the wash after it's been stained! Brilliant. If you are a minimalist at heart, choose a shape that is streamlined. If you can find a sofa that is deep and wide, you won't have to give up comfort. If comfort is everything to you, try a sectional sofa. You can customize sectionals to create the perfect look and feel. You won't get up for days.

 color

Neutral or bold? I tend to choose sofas that are more neutral than bold. Sofas are a big investment, and the last thing you want is to get tired of it too quickly. If the sofa is neutral, you can add pattern and color in the throw pillows, throws, and accent chairs. If there is a color that you have always been drawn to and it's not a trend color for you, then step out of the box and go bold with your sofa.

sofa beds

Sofa beds are a good idea. If you are pressed for space and need an extra place to house your guests, sofa beds are a brilliant solution. They have come a long way from the heavy, boxy styles that used to be so prevalent. You can find modern options that won't scream "sofa bed."

4 Accent Tables

Side tables can be an extension of coffee tables. The one benefit of having a side table butting against a wall is that you can display taller items there and not worry about blocking a view. Side tables should be used for table lamps, taller plants and flowers, and a few smaller items. Use the three- or five-item rule on your table. A perfect ensemble is to group a table lamp with a plant and a small ceramic item.

5 Walls

Have you ever attempted to create a gallery wall and it became an overwhelming task, so much so that you gave up and punched a hole in the wall? Too far-fetched? Not for some people! The key to a good gallery wall is not to take it too seriously. It doesn't need to be perfect by any means. In fact, it should be a little eclectic, a little messy, and a little awesome. For a grouping of small art or tiny art, place each frame about 3 inches apart. The best spacing between normal standard sized frames (that is, sizes 5 × 7, 8 × 10, 11 × 14, 16 × 20, and 24 × 36) is around 4 to 5 inches apart.

You don't necessarily need to create a gallery to fill wall space. Add one or two large pieces of art to bring in color and pattern.

Typography art has been trending for a few years now. It's a great option for bringing some of our own personality into a space. Go easy with it. It's better to use it sparingly than to fill every square inch with words.

The Best
is yet
to Come

Styles of gallery walls

Follow these steps to choose the right style of gallery wall for your home.

portraits

If you have a collection of family photos or even old portrait art, displaying the pictures together is not only stylish but meaningful. When displaying family portraits, mix and match frames for a more relaxed, less staged look. This look is perfect for hallways or to line your staircase walls.

black and white

Black and white is always classic. If you want a look that is less flashy and more classic, choose all black-and-white prints. For an even more cohesive look, choose only black frames or only white frames.

 vintage

Art can create a magical look in your home. Vintage artworks, when grouped together, can feel grand and beautiful. Create a vintage gallery on a focal wall in your living space for immediate style.

4 *frameless*

Displaying art without frames is for the more relaxed, bohemian individual. You can display art using washi tape, simple black tape, or tacks. Use a variety of picture sizes. The more you add to this gallery, the more of a statement it will make.

 photography

Do you have meaningful photographs lying around? Photography makes the best gallery walls! You can even create collections around themes, such as travel, family, buildings, or your animals. The sky's the limit.

specific color palettes

I designed a gallery wall in my living space using black, gold, white, brown, and some greens and blues. It looks cohesive, and each color plays well off the other. Specific color palettes also give a more edited and refined feel. Be sure to keep your frames in the same specific colors as the art.

7 · *tiny art*

If you have a small wall in your home, play off of it and create a tiny art gallery. Flea markets and thrift shops are great sources to find tiny art.

 one frame

Use only one type of frame in different sizes and photos with similar coloring for a subtle, clean gallery. It's perfect for that minimalist home.

6 Sideboard/ Entertainment Center

One topic that comes up almost immediately when talking about living room design is whether or not to have a TV. That preference is completely up to you; the decision may depend on whether or not you also have a family room/media room that can host a TV. It can be a difficult thing to decorate around a TV. Because TVs are big and shiny, you can't really mask them unless you are putting one in a media console or hiding it behind a built-in mirror or art piece. One tip that I have always loved is creating an art gallery around the TV. This can take most of the attention off the TV and onto all of the beautiful art that is displayed.

7 Vignettes

Vignettes, vignettes, vignettes. It's definitely a buzzword right now—a very important one. Vignettes can take your home from normal to magazine ready. When you hear the word *vignette* you may think of a short literary sketch, but in decorating a vignette is a small grouping of objects that creates a pleasing focal point. It's a grouping on top of a table or shelf comprising a variety of different items rather than a large collection of similar items. A vignette creates a focal point that is pleasing to the eye. You can use items that you already own to create a perfect vignette that showcases your life. All you need is a flat surface, such as a dresser, sideboard, shelf, or counter.

Items to use in a vignette:

1   Pottery and ceramic vases

2   Art and photography

3   Plants

4   Mirrors

5   Interesting items from travels

6   Books and magazines

Tips for Creating a Vignette:

1

Build your vignette around a well-lit area.

2

Coordinate with the room by using compatible colors.

3

Display items in odd numbers.

4

Themes can help create consistency.

5

Vary height, depth, and texture.

8 Shelves

Books are a big deal, so bookshelves should be a big deal too. And just because you have a bookshelf, it doesn't mean that every square inch of it should be filled with only books. You can style books alongside a variety of decorative pieces. Stacking books next to a collection of pottery with a plant topping the books is a simple yet beautiful look. Another look is displaying your books vertically with only the spines showing for a neutral look. From there you can layer wood, ceramic, and natural metal accessories. Shelves should be filled with things that you love and that represent you.

Fill your bookshelves with items that you've collected on your travels. This immediately gives your home a sense of culture and personality. Some of my favorite items in my home have been collected over the years from traveling and visiting flea markets and small shops.

9 Rugs

Almost every room needs a rug, especially if the area has hardwood or tile floors. It can be tricky to find the perfect rug for a room. Budget and size seem to always get in the way. If you can splurge, do it. You will not regret having a beautiful rug that brings rich texture and pattern into a space. I have switched out my living room rug at least five times. Every time I do, the room looks completely different. It shows that there is power in the rug.

If you want to add color to a neutral space, add a colorful rug. If you want to keep things simple and more Scandinavian, use a solid neutral rug. Rugs really change everything!

How to arrange your rug:

If your sofa is against the wall, your rug should be large enough to fit under the front legs.

If your living room furniture is floating in the middle of your space, you need a rug that fits under all furniture pieces.

It's better to have a rug that is too large than one that is too small.

■ For more on types of rugs, see page 146.

10 Lighting

I am a firm believer that lighting can make or break a space. Have you ever walked into a space that was a weird orange yellow hue? Or a room that is so badly lit that you can't see in front of you? It's better to have too much lighting than not enough.

The best lighting options for your home:

1   General or ambient lighting acts as the overall lighting of a room. It illuminates all of the room. Ambient lighting fixtures include chandeliers, pendant lights, track lights, and wall sconces.

2   Task lighting lights up a work or reading area. This lighting needs to be brighter than your ambient lighting so that the contrast focuses the light in the specified area.

3   Accent lighting highlights a particular area, like a work of art or a vignette. This lighting creates shadow around the object for a dramatic effect. Sconces and landscape lights are common accent lights.

Dining Room

Dining Room

One of my favorite movies is *Cheaper by the Dozen*, both the 1950 version and the 2003 version. I love the concept of the large family sitting around the dining table. It always makes me want my own large family, just so that I can fill up each chair around the dining table. There's something so nostalgic about dining rooms. Even if we don't necessarily use them every day, they are a place we can host dinner parties, birthday dinners, and large family celebrations. My grandmother always had the stage set perfectly in her dining room. She had a gorgeous dining set with a matching buffet and sideboard. Her china was always washed and ready for guests, and she created the perfect centerpieces for the table. My style doesn't quite lend itself to matchy-matchy, but I do love how invested she was when it came to entertaining and making people feel like they were surrounded by the best of the best. And all of this was on a tight budget. Now, I'm not saying that we should live our lives like June Cleaver from *Leave It to Beaver*. But I am saying that gathering friends and family around a dining table can enable us to pause from the seriousness of life for a moment and bring pure joy to our homes. So we might as well embrace this act of life and create a wonderful scene to host it.

Because dining rooms need the least amount of items, you can invest a little more in this room. And the styling can be a little less stuffy and a lot more thought out than in other rooms. For example, every dining room needs a table, dining chairs, a sideboard for storage, and great lighting. Once those pieces have been established, you can layer items that will create a stylish motif. Art also plays a big part in dining rooms. Use art as a way to bring personality into this space. If you want a dining room that is fun and festive, choose colorful art with lots of movement. If your dining room is a little more clean and sophisticated, stick with neutral pieces of art with simple movement.

*Main areas of your dining room
to be styled:*

1 Sideboards/Buffets

2 Dining Table and Chairs

3 Walls

4 Rug

5 Lighting

1 Sideboards/Buffets

Sideboards are not just useful for storage; they are also a great means of creating beautiful vignettes. Styling vignettes in the dining room can be easy, because you can use dishware and ceramics to decorate a surface. Try stacking white dishes and placing them next to mugs or glassware. Place greenery and plants throughout. Hang art above the vignette, if you need more color and texture.

Styling for a Dinner Party

Bring in greenery from your backyard. Either place the branches in vases or lay them flat for a full effect.

Mix up your dishware. Use vintage and new for a stylish, relaxed look.

Step out and use gold or black flatware instead of the classic silver. You will love the look!

Cloth napkins immediately take a tablescape from blah to mature and awesome.

2 Dining Table and Chairs

Have you ever wondered what to place in the middle of your dining table? We can't always display flowers, and fruit rots if it sits out for too long. One idea is to create a small vignette of candlesticks, flowers, or plants and a favorite bowl. Or how about a large, beautiful ceramic or wooden bowl with nothing in it? Just a simple decorative touch. Another option is to gather a collection of brass candlestick holders and clump them together in the middle of the table.

To have matching dining chairs or to not, that is the question. When you mix your dining chairs, you immediately create a fun, laid-back vibe. When your chairs match, it gives a little more mature and conservative look. This is where your personality can play a factor. Are you a hipster who loves thrift stores and a cold brew, or do you prefer Barneys and all things Chanel? One look that can meet both genres is matching all but the two end chairs. That simple detail can create a stylish yet fun look.

3 Walls

The same rules for the living room can be applied to the dining room. Choose either a gallery wall for major interest or go with a large print.

4 Rugs

Remember to choose a durable rug for your dining area. And make sure that it vacuums easily. You probably don't want to choose a light or shaggy rug. Food and drinks can easily spill, and once that happens you are often stuck with an unsightly stain.

For dining rooms, measure the length and width of your dining table and add 2 feet on each side. Most of the time, dining tables require a rug that's at least 8 feet wide.

5 Lighting

When choosing lighting for your dining room, figure out your needs first and then your wants. Do you need brighter lighting because of the amount of space that you're dealing with? Are you wanting light to be a little more spread out? Pendants and chandeliers come in all shapes and sizes. For the dining room, I always say to go big or go home. Choose something that will make a statement. And whatever you choose, it can be the vehicle to bring color into your space.

Hanging Tips for Your Dining Room Chandelier/ Pendant

1
A chandelier that is hung above a table should have a diameter 1 foot narrower than the table's width. This will prevent any heads hitting the light.

2
Chandeliers should be centered over the dining table, unless you're placing two smaller chandeliers over the table instead of one.

3
A light fixture should be hung 30 to 34 inches above the dining table. You can apply this same rule to kitchen islands.

4
For those super-tall ceilings that are higher than 8 feet, add about 3 inches to the hanging height per foot. If your ceiling is 10 feet tall, your lighting fixture should be hung 36 to 40 inches over the table.

Kitchen

Kitchen

Ah yes, the kitchen—the heart of the home. It's the place that brings us so much joy, the room in which a plethora of people gather in a blink of an eye. The kitchen is and will always be the most loved space in a home. Why? Because we can create magic in it. One of my favorite holidays growing up was Thanksgiving. I loved waking up and smelling the amazing aromas coming from our kitchen.

My mom was a master apple pie baker. Her apple pies were spot-on. Here and there she would use the leftover crust and make what she called snitches, which were small square pieces of buttered crust, sprinkled with cinnamon and sugar. It was the preview to our Thanksgiving dinner. It helped satisfy our appetite while we patiently waited. I could always smell when she started baking the snitches. And of course we kids would start hovering over the oven when that time came. Even if you don't cook or bake, you can always do something in the kitchen. My daily morning kitchen routine involves a pot of coffee and peanut butter toast. I may not be a regular Julia Child, but at least I can enjoy my kitchen.

What makes a kitchen warm and friendly is all of the small details that fill the space. I am the first to condone white, clean kitchens that allow the food to shine bright. But I also love a warm space that doesn't feel sterile. So mixing in accessories that bring in texture and color are of the utmost importance. It can be a bit tricky to style the kitchen. You have to consider appliances, kitchen gadgets, and some details that are less than glamorous, but there are lots of mini tips and tricks that come into account.

*Main areas of your kitchen
to be styled:*

1 Open Shelving

2 Counters

3 Island

4 Lighting

5 Rugs

1 Open Shelving

Open shelving is a way to display all of your beautiful kitchen items. The design arrangement also opens up the room and makes it feel bigger. I've heard clients say that they are wary of having open shelving because they think that dust might accumulate. Yes, dust will gather, but that's nothing a little feather duster and some soap and water can't handle. At my house, we have everyday plates displayed in open shelving; those items are getting used more quickly than they can gather dust.

Note: Do not ignore your window sills. They can become the perfect place to display your smaller plants. Plants need sun anyway, so it's a win-win.

What you can display in open shelving:

1 Dishware

2 Glassware

3 Vases and ceramics

4 Ceramic pots

5 Bowls and trays

6 Mugs

7 Cutting boards

8 Plants (of course)

9 Cookbooks

10 Utensils

■ For a clean, modern look, display only specific items in the same color palette. For instance, use just white dishes, glassware, and a few black ceramic items.

■ For a more eclectic, bohemian look, display a variety of colored and textured ceramic pieces, mixed with wooden items.

■ For an organized look, display your items in collections. Have all dishware on one side and all glassware on the other.

2 Counters

I am a minimalist when it comes to counters. Too much stuff displayed sends me into a tizzy. Some people prefer to hide away any electronic/electric appliance, but that's not always an option for a small kitchen. Kitchen counters can end up hosting a variety of appliances, which then creates a tangle of electric cords, which looks anything less than pretty. It's not realistic to hide all of these items, but there are ways to arrange your essentials while making good use of the surface area you have. It's all about editing. Will you really use that food chopper every day? Is that neon orange canister a necessity? You can always add items later if you've scaled back too much.

Some items to display on your counter:

1   Cutting boards

2   Coffee maker

3   Herb plants

4   A vase full of wooden utensils

5   A bowl of fruit

6   Fresh flowers

7   A modern, clean toaster

3 Island

Kitchen islands don't need a lot of stuff on them. Having too many things can create a cluttered vibe. I suggest keeping it simple with a big wooden bowl or a wicker tray to neatly display stacked dishes or accessories. A large bouquet of fresh flowers is the very best thing for an island. Who doesn't love flowers?

4 Lighting

Kitchens need lighting—good lighting. Who wants to cook in the dark? Start with recessed lighting for an overall wash of light. For island lighting, you will need two or three pendants, unless you choose one large chandelier. And for a light above your sink, choose something small with direct lighting.

The right bulbs to use:

1   **Incandescent bulbs.** These are the traditional bulbs most of us have used over the years. They produce a warm, glowing light.

2   **Compact fluorescent bulbs (CFLs).** These bulbs use 75% less energy and last longer than incandescent bulbs. They usually give off a cool tone, but you can find them in a range of brightness levels.

3   **LEDs (light-emitting diodes).** These bulbs are just as efficient as CFLs, but they can last up to three times longer. Originally they were mostly used for task lighting, because they only provided a harsh, direct light, but they have come a long way since their beginnings. They now offer the same look as incandescents, but they're efficient, they're less hot to the touch, and they last a long time. They are a little pricey, but it's worth it when you take into account the length of their use.

4   **Halogen bulbs.** These give off a bright, white light, similar to natural daylight. They are great for task lighting.

5 Rugs

When choosing a rug for the kitchen, you must think durable and then beautiful. What's the point of a beautiful rug if it just gets trashed? Choose an area rug made from wool or synthetic materials, which have a low pile. Low-pile rugs are more stain-resistant than other weaves, and you can clean them easily with soap and water. If you'll be placing your rug in a high-traffic area, such as in front of the sink, you may want to buy a washable rug that you can throw in the washing machine.

Because kitchens are usually clean, neutral spaces, bringing in a patterned rug seems like the right idea. And if you want to add color to your kitchen but you don't want to paint your cabinets, add a colorful rug to create contrast.

Bathroom

Bathroom

As a designer, one of my favorite spaces to design and style is the bathroom. Bathrooms have come a long way from light strips and teal Formica®. Remember the "orange is everything" bathroom design phase? And let's not forget the horribly fluffy and fuzzy pink toilet lid covers that resided in homes across the world. Did we not consider germs back then? Yuck.

The bathroom design must be considered as well as the design of other rooms in the house. Bad design of this room will affect one's impression of the whole house. For example, a few years back I visited a southern bed-and-breakfast. The foyer into the lobby was absolutely stunning. Each bedroom made you feel warm and cozy, and the dining area was gorgeous, with modernized Americana type decor. And then came the bathrooms. They were brown and yellow with brown linoleum flooring and brown floral wallpaper. Reminder: What happens in the bathroom is already brown and yellow, so stay clear of this color combination.

Nowadays bathroom design is all about creating clean and sanitary spaces that are bright and beautiful. We see lots of ceramic tiles in a variety of colors and shapes. Filling up these bathrooms with small details can be a fun process. Because bathrooms are becoming more and more stylish, the styling aspect has become easier. There's no need to clutter up the bathroom space with decorative items such as small knickknacks and lady figurines made out of porcelain.

*Main areas of your bathroom
to be styled:*

1 Countertop

2 Bathtub

3 Toilet

4 Shelves

5 Lighting

1 Countertop

It's easy to fill your counters with bottles, brushes, and random clutter. Clear the clutter and only display items that are important to you and to your aesthetic. You will love coming into a clean and clutter-free bathroom.

When styling your bathroom counter, use the following items:

1   Trays are perfect for holding bottles and potions.

2   Small baskets or jars can hide items that you don't want to be seen.

3   Tall jars can hold toothbrushes and razors.

4   At thrift stores and flea markets find vintage and ornate bottles to display.

5   Use glass jars for cotton balls and other necessities.

6   Don't throw away beautiful perfume bottles. Use them as a decorative detail.

2 Bathtub

Bathtubs can be tricky to style. A wooden tray or over-the-tub wire rack to place across the width of the tub is great for holding bottles, hand towels, flowers, and candles for a relaxing bubble bath. If your tub doesn't allow for a tray, simply display a few pretty bottles, along with a jar of flowers at the end, and call it good.

3 Toilets

When you have a small bathroom, you need to utilize as much space as you can. One of those areas that can be turned into useable space is behind the toilet. Use a long, narrow tray to display pretty bottles, plants, and other accessories that will add style to your bathroom.

4 Shelves

Open shelves in the bathroom can be a beautiful thing.
It allows for you to show off those items that you love. I have
a collection of bottles from my travels that I've displayed on a
floating shelf above my toilet.

Consider utilizing a large basket or an old wooden crate
to store extra rolls of toilet paper.

Objects to use for open shelving in the bathroom:

1   Vintage bottles

2   Glass bottles with black-and-white typography

3   Perfume bottles

4   Wooden bowls and jars

5   Small plants

6   Unused sugar bowls (These are pretty and can double as storage for small items.)

5 Lighting

Depending on how your bathroom is set up, you will need a couple of lighting options. Start with recessed lighting, and then move to vanity lighting. Vanity lighting is where you can add the wow factor. Whether you are doing sconce lighting or recessed lighting, add a look that will bring instant style to your bathroom.

Vanity lighting ideas:

Hang sconces over the mirror.

Have sconces flank the mirror.

3

Flank the mirror with pendant lights.

Bedroom

Bedroom

Bedrooms seem to become last on the project list, especially master bedrooms. Though we spend half of our days in the bedroom, we still don't make it a priority. When my husband and I bought our first home, we focused on every room but our bedroom. It became a trap for laundry, objects that didn't have a home, and extra furniture that had no purpose. One night while lying in bed, I looked around my bedroom and instantly felt sad. The one room that should act as a sanctuary after a long day became a catchall with no identity. The next day I went on a mission to clean, gut, and organize our bedroom. I took out every single piece of furniture, including the bed, and restructured the entire space. Within twelve hours I had created a little oasis. It didn't cost me anything except some time and effort. Do you ever flip through magazines, see a bedroom that seems to be flawless, and dream of the day that you can achieve a beautiful bedroom? Well, you can have one, and you can do it on a small or big budget. Don't go to bed stressed out because you're surrounded by chaos. Life is hard enough, so why not create a space in which you can feel peace and tranquility?

The first step to creating a stylish, relaxing bedroom is to remove everything and start from scratch. You don't need to buy all new things. It's easier, however, to start with a clean slate and build upon nothing. After you have removed the majority of your things, decide if your furniture configuration is exactly what you want. If you have a large window, try to place your bed where you can look out your window each morning. Or if you have a large space that needs to be decorated, create the perfect sitting area in which you can have your morning coffee.

Once you have created the perfect space plan, start styling your bed. I am all for white or neutral bedding. Hotels do it for a reason, and that reason is to make you feel like you are living in a spa. You might as well create a spalike experience in your own home. If you want to add color or texture to your bed, use a colorful throw blanket, quilt, or a few throw pillows.

Main areas of your bedroom to be styled:

1 Dresser

2 Side table

3 Bed

4 Rug

5 Lighting

1 Dresser

Dressers can be a catchall for accessories, clothes, and other random items.

Five easy steps to create the dresser of your dreams:

1   First, remove everything already on the surface. Also remove anything hanging on the wall.

2   Hang two wall pieces—one functional, one decorative— above the dresser. It will immediately draw the eye upward.

3   Create another layer by stacking books or magazines on the surface. This will also bring in color and pattern.

4   Add personal items, such as plants, jewelry, small jars, and even perfume bottles.

5   For an added bonus, hang a hook off-center from the wall pieces and display your favorite necklaces.

2 Side Tables

Side tables should be kept simple. (There's nothing like knocking things over in the middle of the night.) A few necessities include a table lamp, clock, reading material, candle, ring dish, and a meaningful accessory for some added style. Don't overcomplicate this area. Keep it serene and pretty.

3 Bed

Styling your bed is all about preference. Do you prefer a simple look that includes a quilt, a throw blanket, and maybe a few pillows? Or perhaps you like a little more of a wow factor, which would include color and more than a couple of throw pillows.

When using a variety of patterns, stick to one color palette for a cohesive look. Mixing textures and patterns bring warmth and character into a bedroom.

Some options for bedding looks:

The stylish messy bed. This laid-back style involves a little more wrinkles and a lot less tucked-in sheets. To make it look intentional, fluff your bed pillows and add a few throw pillows.

The proper bed. Clean lines, tucked-in blankets, and wrinkle-free sheets create a very hotel-like look. You only need a few pillows and possibly a throw blanket at the end to complete this look.

The young, hip bed. This look falls between the proper bed and the stylish messy bed. Layer the bed by tucking in the sheets and throwing a quilt on the top. Add a small variety of colored and textured pillows.

4 Rug

Rugs are optional in the bedroom. The biggest reason for adding a rug is to bring in warmth. When placing a rug under your bed, extend it from the bottom two-thirds of the bed.

5 Lighting

Whether you are retiring to a small, cozy bedroom or a large master suite, you most likely need a dose of warm, serene lighting. Dark bedrooms are great for sleeping, but light is still required to accomplish your day-to-day tasks. Table lamps or sconces flanking the bed are both important for late-night reading, but they should not be the only lights in your bedroom. You may want to consider installing recessed lights, a good choice for ambient lighting in any room. Another option that brings in more style is a single flush-mount pendant or chandelier. Supplement your overhead lighting with table lamps, or install hanging lights or wall lights with swing arms over the tables to free up space for books.

To create more mood in your bedroom, place your ambient lighting on dimmer switches that you can adjust. Softer bulbs can also keep your bedroom light from being too bright and unpleasant.

Do you have artwork or photographs on one wall of your bedroom? You might consider having accent lighting there.

Tips for Good Lighting

Place a floor lamp at the end or side of your room so that it doesn't block any view.

Light at least three corners of the room. You can focus one of those lights on an object, like a vignette or piece of art.

Use a variety of table lamps and floor lamps, some with a downward glow and some with an upward glow.

4

Embrace the dimmer. If you have an overhead fixture, put it on a dimmer for mood lighting at night.

Entryway

Entryway

When guests walk into your home, what are they immediately greeted by? Is it a pile of shoes? A sideboard with mail, keys, and other random items scattered about? Or perhaps you have a bench with some hooks for coats and umbrellas? Whatever it is, it's the first impression you are giving your guests. I've always battled with entryways. How do we keep them beautiful yet practical? We all have busy lives, and we all need to think practically, right? Unless you have a twenty-four-hour housekeeper, it's not like you have the luxury of throwing a scarf on the floor and it magically makes its way to a hook. A good entryway should be well edited. It should allow for quick dashes out the door, keys in hand, and make-up checked.

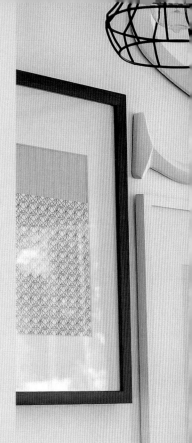

Key elements for making your entryway awesome:

1 The right-sized table—not too big or too small

2 A chair or bench for putting shoes on

3 Lighting to bring your guests out of the dark

4 A mirror for touch-ups on the go

5 A small dish for keys and coins

6 Decorative accessories to bring in style, such as ceramics, plants, art, and pottery

A rug in the entryway is both functional and decorative. It helps to keep your home clean by preventing mud, snow, and other traces of adverse weather from being tracked throughout the house. Your entryway rug should be chosen carefully, for the decorative statement it makes is a visitor's first experience of your personal style.

Types of rugs to choose from:

1   Wool is perfect for high-traffic areas.

2   Silk is beautiful but less sturdy than other fabrics.

3   Cotton is strong yet gathers dirt easily.

4   Jute is great for both indoor and outdoor carpets.

5   Kilim is colorful and beautiful.

6   Distressed rugs give the perfect worn look.

7   Tufted rugs are patterned and less sturdy than other types of rugs.

Kid's Room

Kid's Room

When my kids were first born, I spent hours decorating their nurseries. I wanted everything to be perfect. I wanted it to look like something out of a magazine. The design remained untouched during the first several months. It was perfect. And then they became toddlers. Everything changed. I had to start placing breakable items on higher shelves. No longer could I have valuable art hanging on the walls. Their rooms became mini gymnasiums. My son was a climbing monkey. He would hang off anything in arm's reach. In all of these transitions, I didn't want my kids' bedrooms or playroom to lose style. I firmly believe that we can have both beauty and practicality in one space. Decorating a kid's room doesn't mean you have to scrimp on style. In fact, it opens up a fun new world of bright design possibilities. It allows us to make bold moves and create spaces where the imagination can run wild. Go big, or go home!

Tips for creating the perfect kids' space

Children are creative and innovative. They should hang out in spaces that are filled with imagination, color, and joy-filled details. Here are a few simple tips for you to introduce in your child's space.

1 *color*

Involve your children in the process. Let them choose specific colors, and then work around those colors, even if color is introduced only in a throw pillow or a stuffed animal. It's their room, and they will feel like a million bucks if you ask them for their opinion.

furniture

Quality is much more important than quantity. High-quality pieces will stand the test of time and will provide more design greatness and less of a cheap assembly-line look. For example, look for adaptability like a toddler bed that converts into a twin bed, or versatile styling that could work in other rooms of the house.

 accessorize

Add color with accessories. You can always switch out throw pillows, art, rugs, hooks, and even stuffed animals. Choose fun and cheerful items that will add that kidlike aspect to your stylish space.

theme

Avoid the theme-park trend. Stay clear of items with images of a branded TV show or movie characters. Though your kids love Disney movies, must their rooms be decorated like Disneyland? Stick with themed toys and books.

 storage

Make storage easy. Don't overcomplicate storage, because in the end you will find huge messes due to the difficulty of putting something away in its right place.

Style with
What
You Have

One huge misperception of styling your house is that you have to go on a shopping spree and get all new accessories. *This is so wrong!* A home is supposed to be full of memories and personality. This becomes possible when you use items that you already have and mix them with newer accessories. The following pages show items that you probably have lying around your home that you can and should use to style your space.

① books

Books are the simplest way to bring in class and style. There are many ways to arrange and style books. The most popular method is to mix up the placement. Try a mix of vertical and horizontal arrangements. Do this within the same shelf, and then also try mixing up the way entire shelves are arranged so that one shelf is all horizontal and another is all vertical. Another popular solution is to arrange them by color. You can create a cool, rainbow look with this easy idea. And if you don't want any color, turn your books backward for a neutral look.

2 *family treasures*

Do you have a quirky ceramic bird passed down from your great aunt? Or maybe an embellished vase from your grandmother? Use these items (sparingly) to bring in character to a simple vignette.

 bottles, vessels, and vases

I have a closet full of all of these that I keep on hand for dinner parties, birthday parties, and holidays. I love using fresh flowers any time that I have the chance, so having enough vases on hand is very important.

④ *family pictures*

I don't usually display family pictures in my home, but when the holidays come around, I get really sentimental and start pulling out the baby pictures to place in different vignettes around my house.

 blankets and throws

You never know when you may want an extra pop of color or pattern in your space. Throws and blankets are the perfect way to add something special without having to change your entire room. You can use throws to cover benches and even coffee tables.

magazines

Just as with books, magazines are an easy fix for filling open space. Just stack them, and place decorative items on top or side by side.

The Best
is yet
to Come

artwork

I rarely get rid of my art. You just never know when you are going to want to create an art gallery or when you will want to add art to a blank wall. Art is essential to bring personality, as well as color and texture, to the room. This is very important.

 ceramics and pottery

They can add instant color and pattern to a vignette or tabletop.

9 *plants*

They immediately give a space life and color. Plants can go in any room and can be moved around constantly.

candlesticks

This is a great accessory to add height to vignettes. You can mix and match metals and colors, or keep it cohesive.

Style with What You Found on Your Journey

I say this all of the time: A happy home is a well-traveled home. That doesn't mean that you need to travel to far-off places just to find things with which to style your home. A nearby state will do. Just make sure that you are picking up items along your journey that mean something, that bring back wonderful memories, and that are significant to you and your loved ones. Have you ever walked into a home that felt like a Pottery Barn® or an Ikea® showroom? Where everything was chosen from one store and it just felt sterile? Life can be hard enough without having to worry about our homes being sad and lifeless. Bringing in nostalgic items can give a look as stylish as bringing in an entire truck full of Hay® furniture.

My grandparents lived in a humble mobile home when I was growing up. It was on a beautiful piece of property with lots of trees, many cows, and a flock of chickens. It wasn't a mansion by any means, but my grandmother made it feel as if it were. She filled that home with beautiful items that she had

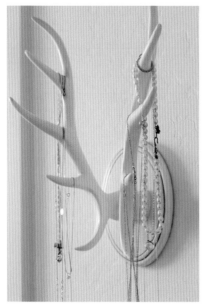

collected over the years. Family heirloom pictures and accessories were scattered about. Artworks that my great-uncles had painted were always hung with such pride.

My grandmother took such care of her home. She created not just a showroom, but a home. It felt important to her to live a life surrounded by not just beauty but also memories and happiness.

Resources

Here's a list of some of my favorite resources for all things styling!

accessories

A+R
www.aplusrstore.com

Anthropologie
www.anthropologie.com

Far & Wide Collective
www.farandwidecollective.com

The Land of Nod
www.landofnod.com

Local and Lejos
www.localandlejos.com

Menu
www.menu.as

Minimal
www.minimal.com

Royal Design
www.royaldesign.com

Schoolhouse Electric
www.schoolhouseelectric.com

Target
www.target.com

Tictail
tictail.com/market

To the Market
www.tothemarket.com

Urban Outfitters
www.urbanoutfitters.com

art

Art
www.art.com

Art Crate
www.artcrate.co

I Love My Type
www.ilovemytype.com

Jaime Derringer
www.jaimederringer.com

Minted
www.minted.com

Olleeksell
www.olleeksell.tictail.com

The Poster Club
www.theposterclub.com

furniture

Apt 2B
www.apt2b.com

Bludot
www.bludot.com

Bryght
www.bryght.com

Crate&Barrel
www.crateandbarrel.com

Design Public
www.designpublic.com

DotandBo
www.dotandbo.com

Dwell Studio
www.dwellstudio.com

Ferm Living
www.fermliving.com

Homestead Seattle
www.homesteadseattle.com

Joss & Main
www.jossandmain.com

Lexmod
www.lexmod.com

Lulu&Georgia
www.luluandgeorgia.com

Menu
www.menu.as

Modani
www.modani.com

Mutto
www.muuto.com

Normann-Copenhagen
www.normann-copenhagen.com

Overstock
www.overstock.com

PB Teen
www.pbteen.com

Restoration Hardware
www.restorationhardware.com

Room and Board
www.roomandboard.com

Rove Concepts
www.roveconcepts.com

True Modern
www.truemodern.com

2 modern
www.2modern.com

Wayfair
www.wayfair.com

West Elm
www.westelm.com

Yliving
www.yliving.com

lighting

Armadillo-co
www.armadillo-co.com

Barn Light Electric
www.barnlightelectric.com

Bludot
www.bludot.com

The Citizenry
www.the-citizenry.com

DotandBo
www.dotandbo.com

Royal Design
www.royaldesign.com

Foscarini
www.lightology.com

Ikea
www.ikea.com

The Land of Nod
www.landofnod.com

PB Teen
www.pbteen.com

Restoration Hardware
www.restorationhardware.com

Schoolhouse Electric
www.schoolhouseelectric.com

Target
www.target.com

Triple Seven
www.triplesevenhome.com

West Elm
www.westelm.com

rugs

Dwell Studio
www.dwellstudio.com

H&M Home
www.hm.com

Homestead Seattle
www.homesteadseattle.com

Ikea
www.ikea.com

One Kings Lane
www.onekingslane.com

PB Teen
www.pbteen.com

Solo Rugs
www.solorugs.com

Urban Outfitters
www.urbanoutfitters.com

West Elm
www.westelm.com

World Market
www.worldmarket.com

Yliving
www.yliving.com

textiles

Arro Home
www.arrohome.com

By Molle
www.bymolle.com

Canvas Home Store
www.canvashomestore.com

The Citizenry
www.the-citizenry.com

Cotton and Flax
www.cottonandflax.com

Coveted Home
www.covetedhome.com

Deny Designs
www.denydesigns.com

Design Public
www.designpublic.com

Design Within Reach
www.dwr.com

Dwell Studio
www.dwellstudio.com

Far & Wide Collective
www.farandwidecollective.com

Fashionable
https://livefashionable.com

Ferm Living
www.fermliving.com

Happy Habitat
www.happyhabitat.net

Heather Winn Bowman
www.heatherwinnbowman.com

Jaymee Srp
www.jaymeesrp.com

Local and Lejos
www.localandlejos.com

Louise Gray
www.louisegray.com

Shop Territory Design
www.shopterritorydesign.com

Society 6
https://society6.com

To the Market
www.tothemarket.com

Zara Home
www.zarahome.com/us/en-us/

wallpaper

Chasing Paper
www.chasingpaper.com

Cole and Son
www.cole-and-son.com

Ferm Living
www.fermliving.com

Makelike
www.makelike.com

Walls Need Love
www.wallsneedlove.com

Acknowledgments

Some major thank-yous go to the following people. Paige French who immediately saw my vision and photographed the heck out of each space. THANK YOU! Diana Ventimiglia and the Sterling Publishing team who saw potential in me and gave me this life-changing opportunity. Janna Smith for the being the best assistant that anyone could wish for. Jenn Lee who helped me gain confidence in my writing. To the following families for letting me invade their amazing homes for this book: Barths, Krens, Fishers, Salinas's, Sewards, Coffields, Vaughns, Loubeks, Smiths, Eisens, Johnsons, and McFerrins. You're all simply the best. To all of my friends and family, near and far, who have constantly encouraged me through this small journey. To my mom, who has prayed me through storms and celebrations. To my two kids who are my little angels sent from heaven. To my incredibly hot husband who married me 16 years ago and has been my best friend ever since. To Jesus who continues to be my confidant.

About the Author

Interior stylist *Kirsten Grove* has always had a passion for interior design. Today Kirsten uses her blog *Simply Grove* as a creative outlet for all things aesthetically beautiful. Started in 2008 as a way to show off eye-catching design and decor from all over the world, *Simply Grove* has become a hangout for like-minded creatives with a love of interiors and an appetite for design eye-candy. Kirsten has styled and designed for clients all over the world. Her most recent projects have included residences in Stockholm, commercial property in Seattle, and more residences in New York City, Los Angeles, and Denver.

Don't be surprised if you have bumped into Kirsten (as a contributor) on such publications and sites as *Better Homes and Gardens*, Hayneedle.com, *Interior Collective* by Caesarstone, Martha Stewart.com, and *2Modern*. She has also been featured in magazines such as *Better Homes and Gardens*, *Gray*, *Lucky*, *The Nest*, and *Real Living*; blogs such as *Apartment Therapy*, *decor8*, *Design*Sponge*, and

Wedding Chicks; and websites such as Elle Decor .com, HGTV.com, and Martha Stewart.com. She was also named one of *Better Homes and Gardens* top 10 best decorating blogs as well as Babble's Top 50 Design Mom Bloggers of 2011 and has been a speaker at Alt Summit 2011, 2012, and 2013, as well as other conferences around the United States. Kirsten has collaborated with major companies such as eBay, GMC, Lowe's, Nissan, Pottery Barn, and Sherwin-Williams.

Kirsten offers a full design service, including e-decorating (which is done completely online), home styling, new construction design, commercial designing, and other design-related services. Email Kirsten at kirsten@simplygrove.com.

Index

(continued on the following page)

(continued on the following page)